THE TERRIBLE FATE OF HUMPTY DUMPTY

David Calcutt

OXFORD
UNIVERSITY PRESS

OXFORD
UNIVERSITY PRESS

Great Clarendon Street, Oxford, OX2 6DP, United Kingdom

Oxford University Press is a department of the University of Oxford.
It furthers the University's objective of excellence in research, scholarship,
and education by publishing worldwide. Oxford is a registered trade mark of
Oxford University Press in the UK and in certain other countries

First published by Thomas Nelson and Sons Ltd in 1986
Second edition published by Nelson Thornes Ltd in 2012
This edition published by Oxford University Press in 2014

British Library Cataloguing in Publication Data
Data available

978-1-4085-1996-7

6

Printed in Great Britain

Acknowledgements
Illustrations: John James
Page make-up: Malcolm Smythe
Designed and produced: Bender Richardson White

CONTENTS

SERIES EDITOR'S INTRODUCTION

Dramascripts is an exciting series of plays especially chosen for students in the lower and middle years of secondary school. The titles range from the best in modern writing to adaptations of classic texts such as *A Christmas Carol* and *Silas Marner.*

Dramascripts can be read or acted purely for the enjoyment and stimulation that they provide; however, each play in the series also offers all the support that pupils need in working with the text in the classroom:

- **Introduction** – this offers important background information and explains something about the ways in which the play came to be written.
- **Script** – this is clearly set out in ways that make the play easy to handle in the classroom.
- Notes explain references that pupils might not understand, and language points that are not obvious.
- **Activities** – at the end of scenes, acts or sections – give pupils the opportunity to explore the play more fully. Types of activity include: discussion, writing, hot-seating, improvisation, acting, freeze-framing, story-boarding and artwork.
- **Looking Back at the Play** – this section has further activities for more extended work on the play as a whole with emphasis on characters, plots, themes and language.

AUTHOR'S INTRODUCTION

In the early 1980s, for about a four years, I ran a theatre group called Forest Youth Theatre, which was based at a community school in Walsall in the West Midlands. The majority of its members – aged 13–18 – lived on the large estate that served the school. Although I was both the writer and director for the group, our method of working was very much a collaborative one. We used techniques of devising and improvisation to develop ideas for themes and characters and scenes: we gradually worked on the ideas in a more and more structured way until they were no longer improvisations but shaped and crafted pieces of theatre.

It was this method we used, in 1984, to develop a play about bullying, and which dealt with themes and ideas close to the lives and experiences of the group's members. From the start, we wanted the structure of the play to be in the form of an investigation into a tragedy – in this case, the tragedy of a boy's death as a result of bullying. But, the more we worked on developing the play, the more it became not only an investigation into the facts surrounding the boy's death, but into human nature itself, and how we so often fail to recognise a dangerous, damaging, and potentially lethal situation until it's too late – which could be one definition of tragedy.

Our aim in working on the play, and my aim in writing the final version, was not to bang any particular social or ideological drum, nor to offer any simple solution to the tragedy of the story. Drama doesn't work like that, and it's not what it's for. The play illuminates a particular group of characters who become involved in a particular sequence of events. From the outset, we know the story is a tragic one, and we observe and become involved with those characters as they are driven, almost against their own wills, towards the tragedy, not only of Terry's fate, but of the revelation of their own weaknesses and failings. But it's always been my feeling, and it still is, that this is not a despairing play. In recognising our failures, in coming to understand that we all share some responsibility for what happens to others, there lies the potential for the growth of the mind, the heart, and the spirit. And in that potential there is hope.

The Characters

TERRY DUMPTON	quiet, reserved, the gang's victim
STUBBS	powerful, intelligent, the gang leader
JIMMY	gang-member, a bit of a thug, not very bright
PETE	gang-member, a joker
KATHY	gang-member, tough
KAY	gang-member, tough
JANET	gang-member, scared of the others
TRACEY	gang-member, scared of the others
SAMMY	Terry's friend, weak, hanger-on of the gang
POLICE OFFICER 1	
POLICE OFFICER 2	
MRS DUMPTON	Terry's mother, strong, the family's breadwinner, in her 30s
MR DUMPTON	Terry's father, out of work, in his 30s
LESLEY DUMPTON	Terry's younger sister, aged about 8
ROSS WEBSTER	local press reporter, ambitious, in his early 20s
MRS VICKERS	witness, in her mid-40s, a little vain
THE HEAD TEACHER	woman, in her early 40s, defensive
MRS WILLIAMS	aquaintance of Mrs Dumpton, in her 30s
MRS CLARK	Janet's mother, friend of Mrs Williams, in her 30s

The play was originally written for, and performed by, Forest Youth Theatre in June 1984.

Production Note: Although the play is, for the purposes of reading and rehearsal, divided into scenes, it was written with the intention of a continual performance, with action and events flowing without break from beginning to end. It was also intended that the play could be staged with a minimum of props, costume and staging. At its simplest, all that's necessary, is an empty, open space, and strong, committed performances.

THE TERRIBLE FATE OF HUMPTY DUMPTY
SCENE 1

(On waste ground. STUBBS, with THE MEMBERS OF HIS GANG – JIMMY, PETE, KATHY, KAY, JANET and TRACEY – are surrounding TERRY DUMPTON. SAMMY stands to one side. THE GROUP suddenly comes to life as the introductory music fades.)

PETE *(To TERRY.)* See my frisbee, Humpty? My best frisbee, this is. I've had this frisbee for ages. I love it. I'd hate to lose it. I'd go mad if I lost this frisbee. Want to see how it works? . . .   1

(PETE throws the frisbee into the air. Then he says:)

. . . Oh, dear. It's got stuck in the pylon. What am I going to do now?

STUBBS You'll have to get it back, Pete.

PETE I know. Only trouble is, I'm scared of heights. Can't stand them. I get a nosebleed just going to the top of the stairs.

STUBBS You'll have to get somebody to fetch it down for you, then.   10

PETE That's right. Who, though?

(STUBBS points at TERRY.)

STUBBS Him! . . .

(There is a pause. Then STUBBS says)

. . . All right, Humpty? Up you go. Get Pete's frisbee back for him . . .

(There is tension. Then STUBBS continues)

... Go on. Climb the pylon. Get it back ...

(TERRY stares up at the pylon. STUBBS goes on)

... Perhaps you ain't our mate, then. Perhaps you don't like us at all. That means you're the kind of person who'd sneak on us.

(He walks towards TERRY.)

TERRY   All right, I'll get it.

SAMMY   Don't, Terry.

STUBBS   Shurrup, Sammy.

SAMMY   It's dangerous.

KATHY   You wanna go up there instead?

(There is a pause.)

STUBBS   Go on.

(TERRY starts to climb the pylon. Egged on by PETE, THE MEMBERS OF THE GANG start to chant 'Humpty Dumpty!' over and over again, and then shout comments up at TERRY.

SAMMY runs forward.)

SAMMY   Don't, Terry. Come down.

---

sneak *'tell' This is a challenge to Terry: either he's with the gang or he's against them. Terry takes up the challenge and climbs the poylon to show he wants to be with the gang. Sammy does tell about them later. The tragedy of the play might have been averted if he'd told sooner.*

Shurrup *slang for 'shut up'.*

Lights suddenly flash on and off. *This represents the the flash of electricity from the cables. In reaching for the frisbee, Sammy puts his hand too close to the cable, causing the massive amount of electricity running through the cables to leap accross the short gap and surge through his body, killing him instantly.*

STUBBS   Shurrup, Sammy, unless you wanna go up there after him.

(The noise continues. Lights suddenly flash on and off. TERRY hangs dead from the pylon. THE MEMBERS OF THE GANG stare up in silence.)

40

 DISCUSSION: As a class, discuss what effect you think this opening scene might have on an audience. Why do you think the author decides to open the play with this particular scene.

DISCUSSION: In groups of two, find lines which indicate that Stubbs is the leader of this gang, and find lines which show that Sammy is sympathetic to Terry.
   Or in groups of three take on the roles of Stubbs, Sammy and Pete, and tell the story of what happens in this scene from your point of view.

SCENE 2

(THE MEMBERS OF THE GANG turn away from the pylon. They are excited and scared.)

JIMMY	Stubbs, what we gonna do?
JANET	Did you see him?
TRACEY	He was just hanging there.
PETE	Perhaps he's having us on. Just a joke, you know.
KATHY	Don't be stupid. You saw the flash.
TRACEY	It was an accident. That's what it was, wasn't it? It was just an accident.
KAY	Course, yeah. That's all it was. Just an accident.
PETE	He was hanging there. Just hanging there. Like a fried egg! A fried egg! Get it?
	(PETE laughs.)
JIMMY	Shurrup, will you? Stop laughing. I said stop laughing!
	(He pushes PETE.)
PETE	Gerroff, Jimmy.
JIMMY	Stop laughing, then, will you?
PETE	All right. I've stopped.
KATHY	Will you two stop it?

1

A fried egg! *Pete's sick joke makes a reference to Terry's nickname, 'Humpty Dumpty' – that nursery ryhme character being an egg. The audience isn't aware yet of this nickname.*

PETE	It's him, throwing his weight around.
KATHY	Just stop it. You're getting on my nerves.
KAY	And mine.
JIMMY	What we gonna do, Stubbs? Tell us. What we gonna do?
JANET	I want to go home. I don't want to stay here. I'm going home.
KATHY	No, you ain't. You're staying here.
JANET	You can't stop me.
KATHY	Want a bet?
KAY	Yeah. Want to bet?
STUBBS	Will you all just shurrup? I'm trying to think.
KATHY	It's about time.
STUBBS	And you, Kathy. Knock it off. We gotta think what to do.
TRACEY	It was an accident, wasn't it. It wasn't our fault.
STUBBS	That's right. It was an accident. It wasn't nothing to do with us. We wasn't even here.
JIMMY	What do you mean, Stubbs? We was here.
PETE	Listen to what he's got to say, thickhead.
JIMMY	Don't call me thickhead.
KATHY	For God's sake, will you two shurrup?
STUBBS	Right. Listen. This is the story. We wasn't here. We was somewhere else. Down the town. Right? We don't know what happened. We don't know anything about it. Anybody asks us, that's what we tell them. We wasn't here.
KATHY	That's your idea, is it?
STUBBS	Yeah. Why? You got a better one?

20

30

40

PETE	What about my frisbee?
STUBBS	Your what?
PETE	My frisbee.
TRACEY	Dumpton's dead, and all he can think about is his frisbee.
PETE	It's important. My frisbee's still up there.
STUBBS	Has it got your name on it?
PETE	No . . .
STUBBS	Well, it don't matter, then, does it?
JIMMY	Thickhead.
JANET	We ought to phone for an ambulance. We ought to tell somebody.
PETE	Ambulance ain't no good for him now. It's a hearse he needs.
JANET	You're sick, you are.
TRACEY	Janet's right. We ought to tell somebody. The police.
STUBBS	We ain't telling nobody!
JANET	We can't just leave him up there.
STUBBS	You wanna drop us all in it? Is that what you want? You know what'll happen if they find out.
KATHY	Stubbs is right. We've all gotta stick together now. Stick to the same story. That's the only thing we can do.
KAY	Yeah. That's right.
STUBBS	Everybody agreed, then? Right?
JANET	I suppose so. As long as I can go home. I don't feel very well.
KATHY	You can go home now. Just make sure you don't say anything.

50

60

70

JANET	I won't.
TRACEY	I'm coming with you.
	(JANET and TRACEY go.)
PETE	I'm going as well. See you tomorrow.
STUBBS	See you, Pete.
	(PETE goes.)
KATHY	*(Pointing to SAMMY.)* What about him?
STUBBS	Leave him to me. He won't be no trouble.
KATHY	Just make sure of it.
STUBBS	I will!
KATHY	Come on, Kay.
	(KATHY and KAY go.)
STUBBS	You got the story straight, Sammy?
SAMMY	What?
STUBBS	Got the story? We weren't here.
SAMMY	We killed him.
STUBBS	I'm warning you.
SAMMY	We killed him. It was us. We did that.
STUBBS	Jimmy. See to him . . .
	(JIMMY grabs SAMMY. Then STUBBS says)

80

90

. . . Now listen, Sammy. You're in this with the rest of us. So don't you go talking to anybody about it. Right? 'Cos if you do, it ain't just the police you'll have to worry about. You'll have to worry about Jimmy here making such a mess of your face that nobody'll ever recognise you again. They won't even know if you was a human being. Ain't that right, Jimmy?

JIMMY	Yeah. That's right.

STUBBS   So just remember, Sammy. Remember whose side you're on . . .   10

(There is a pause. Then STUBBS says)

. . . Come on, Jimmy.

(JIMMY looses SAMMY.)

JIMMY   Remember, Sammy.

(STUBBS and JIMMY go. Then SAMMY looks up at TERRY'S body.)

SAMMY   Terry . . . I'm sorry . . . I tried to help but . . . I'm sorry . . .

(He faces THE AUDIENCE, and says)

. . . We killed him!

(He runs off.)   11

DISCUSSION: As a class, discuss what you have learned at the end of these two scenes about the members of the gang? For example, what does Stubbs say that shows he is the leader? What can we tell about the others from the kind of things they say?

FREEZE-FRAMING: In a group of eight, create a freeze-frame for the end of Scene 1, as the gang-members stare up at Terry's body. In turn, each of you say what your character is thinking at that particular moment.

SCENE 3

(TWO POLICE OFFICERS enter.)

FIRST POLICE OFFICER Having ascertained that the corpse was that of a Terry 1
Richard Dumpton, aged 14, of 6 Richmond Road, we
proceeded to that address under the direction of the
Inspector, to inform the parents of the deceased of his
death, and also to question them as to the possible
circumstances under which the death may have occurred.
We arrived at number 6 Richmond Road, at 8.14 p.m.; and
there informed the parents.

SECOND POLICE OFFICER Despite the obvious distress to his parents, Mrs Dumpton
in particular proved to be extremely cooperative, and 10
attempted to answer our questions as best she could. She
also agreed to accompany us to the station, where she made
a statement.

*(During this speech, MRS DUMPTON has entered. She is shown
to a seat by THE FIRST POLICE OFFICER.)*

MRS DUMPTON I told him. I said something would happen. I knew there'd

*In this scene, the police officers are, in effect, speaking what would be their
written statements on the case. This leads into Mrs Dumpton making her own
statement. The scenes that follow are all 'illustration' of her statement to the
police. The events in this scene – the parents being informed, Mrs Dumpton
making a statement at the police station – would probably take place over a
number of days. For dramatic and theatrical purposes, they are compressed
into one short scene.*

*Having ascertained . . . and **the parents of the deceased** . . . 'Having
confirmed or discovered the identity of . . . and the parents of the one who's
dead . . .' The unemotional dry language of the police distances them, and us,
from the horror of what's happened. Suddenly, Terry's death is just another
case to be dealt with.*

be some kind of trouble some day. It was them kids at school, that gang. I bet they're at the back of all this. He'd never tell us anything about it. He was a quiet boy, very nervous. That's why they picked on him, I suppose.   2●

FIRST POLICE OFFICER   Who were these children?

MRS DUMPTON   Children from his school. A gang.

SECOND POLICE OFFICER   Do you know their names?

MRS DUMPTON   No. He wouldn't talk about them, like I said. He was scared of them. They terrified him. And now they've gone and killed him.

FIRST POLICE OFFICER   I think it's a bit early to go making accusations like that, Mrs Dumpton.

SECOND POLICE OFFICER   We know nothing about this so-called gang. We don't know that anyone else was there when your son died.   3●

MRS DUMPTON   My Terry wasn't the sort of boy to go doing things like that on his own. Climbing pylons. What would he want to go climbing pylons for, unless they made him?

FIRST POLICE OFFICER   There was a frisbee lodged in the pylon as well.

MRS DUMPTON   A frisbee? My Terry didn't have a frisbee. It wasn't his. You

Children from his school. A gang. *The drama of this play centres around the power of The Gang. The gang in this play is typical of most. It has its own internal power structure and hierarchy: leader, leader's side-kicks, thugs, hangers on and, of course, the reasons for the gang's existence, a victim. Gangs operate on all levels of society, from the playground to the political arena. An examination of Hitler's power structure in Nazi Germany, Stalin's in Communist Russia, or that of any organisation that uses naked power to gain its end, would show that they operate in much the same way as Stubbs' gang in the play.*

	see! You find out about this gang. You go up to his school. You'll see that they're behind this.
SECOND POLICE OFFICER	Of course, we'll make the fullest enquiries, Mrs Dumpton.
MRS DUMPTON	You see that you do. I want them found out. I want them found out and punished for killing my son!
FIRST POLICE OFFICER	If anyone's responsible, we'll find them . . .

(He pauses and then says)

. . . You could help us by answering a few questions.

SECOND POLICE OFFICER	Where did your son say he was going tonight?
MRS DUMPTON	We didn't see him. He didn't come home from school. He was often late. I think he used to come home the long way, to try and keep out of the way of those bullies.
FIRST POLICE OFFICER	These . . . bullies. Do you know anything about them?
MRS DUMPTON	Not much. Terry was too scared to talk about them. It was only when we noticed his strange behaviour that we thought something was wrong. Ever since we moved into the area we've had nothing but trouble. Ever since Terry went to that school. He changed from the first day.
SECOND POLICE OFFICER	How did he change?

40

50

bullies *The word belies the real terror caused by the action of bullies. Bullying thrives on fear of physical pain, leading to often massive mental and psycological stress. A child who's being bullied over a long period of time lives a nightmare existence. And it is fear and shame that keeps the victim from telling anyone what's happening – and so ensures that the bullying continues, and grows worse.*

MRS DUMPTON   It's hard to say. He was just acting . . . strange. You know. Quieter than usual. And coming home late. We asked him about it one evening . . .

(THE POLICE OFFICERS step back and observe the scene.)

DISCUSSION: In pairs, discuss the reasons Mrs Dumpton gives for believing Terry was being bullied.

HOT-SEATING: Mrs Dumpton has just received terrible news. How do you think she feels? She may have a number of conflicting feelings. In groups of four, one of you take on the role of Mrs Dumpton, and the other three ask her questions to find out what her feelings are.

WRITING: Begin to make notes on the different characters in the play. You can add to these notes as the play develops; add new characters as they appear so that you will have a collection of 'character profiles'.

DISCUSSION: In pairs, discuss why Mrs Dumpton is concerned about Terry's behaviour.

SCENE 4

(MR DUMPTON enters and goes to speak to HIS WIFE.)

MRS DUMPTON	He's late again, Arthur.	1
MR DUMPTON	He's still not home?	
MRS DUMPTON	No. It's half-past five.	
MR DUMPTON	I'd better have a word with him when he gets in.	
MRS DUMPTON	Don't be hard on him, Arthur. I think there's something wrong. He's been acting ever so strange lately.	
MR DUMPTON	You don't have to tell me that.	
MRS DUMPTON	I'm getting quite worried about him. He's not been the same since he started at that new school.	
MR DUMPTON	Perhaps he's just taking time to settle down.	10
MRS DUMPTON	I think it's more than that.	
MR DUMPTON	Well. We'll see.	
MRS DUMPTON	Look, I'll have to go. I've got to get to work. Lesley's upstairs playing in the bedroom. Don't forget she's got to have her bath tonight.	
MR DUMPTON	I won't.	
MRS DUMPTON	Your tea's in the oven. 'Bye, Arthur.	
MR DUMPTON	'Bye . . .	

(MRS DUMPTON goes, and MR DUMPTON sits down. After a moment, TERRY comes in, and MR DUMPTON says to him) 20

	. . . Hallo, son.
TERRY	Hallo.

MR DUMPTON	Seen your Mum?
TERRY	No.
MR DUMPTON	She's just this minute gone out . . .
	(He looks closely at TERRY, and says)
	. . . You must've missed her . . .
	(TERRY sits down, and HIS FATHER asks)
	. . . Just got in?
TERRY	Yeah.
MR DUMPTON	Bit late, isn't it?
TERRY	Dunno.
MR DUMPTON	It's twenty to six! . . .
	(There is a brief silence. Then MR DUMPTON says)
	. . . Your Mum's put your tea in the oven.
TERRY	I'll go and get it in a minute.
	(Another pause. Then)
MR DUMPTON	Where've you been till now, anyway?
TERRY	Nowhere.
MR DUMPTON	What do you mean, nowhere? You must have been somewhere.
TERRY	Just coming home.
MR DUMPTON	It doesn't take two hours to get home from school.
TERRY	I went for a walk.
MR DUMPTON	Where?
TERRY	I dunno, just a walk.
MR DUMPTON	Where did you go for a walk?

TERRY	Just round the town.	
MR DUMPTON	What for?	
TERRY	I wanted to!	50

(A pause.)

MR DUMPTON	Look, Terry. Me and your Mum, we're getting a bit worried about you. I mean, this isn't the first time you've been late home from school. And you've . . . I don't know . . .you've been acting different . . .

(A pause.)

. . . Is there something wrong? Something troubling you? . . .

(A pause.)

. . . Is it the school? Is that it? It'll take a bit of time to settle   60
down . . .

(A pause.)

. . . What's troubling you, Terry?

TERRY	Nothing.
MR DUMPTON	Yes, there is. I'm your father. I know when there's something wrong.
TERRY	No, you don't.
MR DUMPTON	Don't talk to me like that! . . .

(A pause.)

. . . Look, I don't want to have an argument. I don't want to   70
row. I just want you to tell me what's wrong. So I can help.
That's what we're here for, you know . . .

(A pause.)

. . . Tell me, Terry.

	(TERRY stands up.)
TERRY	There ain't nothing wrong. I'm all right.
	(TERRY walks away.)
MR DUMPTON	Where are you going?
TERRY	To get my tea!
MR DUMPTON	Terry! Terry!
	(TERRY does not reply so MR DUMPTON walks off angrily.)

SCENE 5

(MRS DUMPTON comes back.)

MRS DUMPTON   We couldn't get anything out of him. He'd always been   1
such a happy child. Quiet, but happy. We'd always got on
well together as a family. You know, of course, that Mr
Dumpton has got a police record. He was inside for a year.
It was silly, really. He got mixed up in something. But he'd
served his time. That's why we moved to a new area, to try
and leave all that behind. Start a new life. Then all this
trouble started with Terry. If only he'd have talked to us,
told us about what was happening, then this . . . this might
not have happened. I heard him crying quite a few times as   10
well. In his bedroom at night. But when I went in to see
him, he just pretended to be asleep. That's not normal, is it?
For a boy of his age to cry in bed at night. And then there
was the whole thing about the money. That shocked me
more than anything, I can tell you.

HOT-SEATING: In groups of four, hot-seat Mr Dumpton to find out why he gets angry. Is it just Terry that makes him angry, or might there be other reasons as well?

WRITING: Write a list of other situations in which a child might be questioned by a parent, and be reluctant to answer them.

IMPROVISATION: In groups of two, use one of the above situations to improvise a short scene between parent and child.

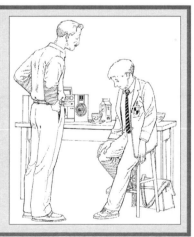

SCENE 6

(LESLEY DUMPTON comes in, spilling her toy bricks over the floor.)

MRS DUMPTON Lesley! Will you clear this stuff up off the floor?

LESLEY I'm playing.

MRS DUMPTON And I'm trying to clear up before I go out. Go and play in your bedroom.

LESLEY I want to play here.

MRS DUMPTON And I want you to go and play in your bedroom.

LESLEY It's messy.

MRS DUMPTON You should tidy it up, then. Now get this stuff cleared up!

LESLEY All right.

(She starts to tidy up.)

1

MRS DUMPTON I don't know where your father is. Or Terry. They should both be home by now.

LESLEY Dad's down the pub, getting drunk.

MRS DUMPTON Don't you be so cheeky, young lady. Of course he isn't down the pub. They're not open yet. Still trying to find himself a job, I suppose. He knows he's supposed to be here by now . . .

(LESLEY has started playing again. HER MOTHER says)

Dad's down the pub . . . *and . . .* **They're not open yet.** *In 1984, when this play was written, pubs opened at lunch-time, then closed around 3pm, and didn't open until 6 or 7 in the evening, unlike the present time with unlimited licensing hours.*

	. . . Lesley! You're supposed to be clearing those up, not playing with them.	20
LESLEY	I am clearing them up.	
MRS DUMPTON	No, you're not. Now take them upstairs.	
LESLEY	All right . . .	
	(She starts to walk away. Then she stops, and says)	
	. . . Mum.	
MRS DUMPTON	What?	
LESLEY	Can I play with Terry's models?	
MRS DUMPTON	No, you cannot.	
LESLEY	Please, Mum.	
MRS DUMPTON	No. You might break them.	30
LESLEY	I won't. Please.	
MRS DUMPTON	You'll have to wait till he gets in and ask him then. If he gets in.	
LESLEY	Thanks, Mum.	
	(LESLEY goes.)	
MRS DUMPTON	I'll be late again for work at this rate . . .	
	(TERRY comes in. HIS MOTHER says to him)	
	. . . There you are. You're late again.	
	(TERRY sits down.)	
TERRY	I know.	40
MRS DUMPTON	Your Dad's not in yet, so you'll have to look after Lesley till he gets here. Your tea's in the oven . . .	
	(A pause. Then MRS DUMPTON asks)	
	. . . Everything all right?	

TERRY	Yeah.
MRS DUMPTON	Sure?
TERRY	Yeah.
MRS DUMPTON	Good. I'll have to get off to work in a minute, I was late yesterday, and the night before that. I don't want to be late again tonight. They'll be giving me my cards, and we can do without that.

5

(LESLEY comes back.)

LESLEY	Terry.
TERRY	What?
LESLEY	Can I play with your models?
TERRY	No.

(LESLEY starts to cry.)

LESLEY	Mum. Terry won't let me play with his models.
MRS DUMPTON	Terry! Let her play with them. She won't break them.
TERRY	No. They're mine.

6

MRS DUMPTON	Look at the fuss she's making.
TERRY	I don't care. They ain't toys. They're models.
MRS DUMPTON	She's crying.
TERRY	Let her cry, then.
LESLEY	You're horrible, you are. I hate you. Big fat pig.

(She runs away.)

They'll be giving me my cards. *This is a reference to the fact that, in earlier times, each employee had a card on which the employer placed their weekly National Insurance stamps. If an employee was sacked from a job, the employer returned this card to the employee to hand over to their next employer.*

MRS DUMPTON	*(To TERRY)* Now look what you've done. You've upset her.
TERRY	I don't care.
MRS DUMPTON	You don't seem to care about anything these days. Well, I can't be bothered with it. I've got to get off. Just get my purse . . .
	(She gets her purse. She looks in it, and then says)
	. . . Terry. Have you seen my money?
TERRY	What money?
MRS DUMPTON	I had six pound notes in this purse last night. Now there's only three . . .
	(TERRY shrugs. HIS MOTHER goes on)
	. . . Are you sure you don't know anything about it?
TERRY	No. Why should I?
MRS DUMPTON	I just thought you might know something.
TERRY	Well, I don't.
	(LESLEY comes back.)
MRS DUMPTON	Lesley. Do you know anything about my money? . . .
	(LESLEY shakes her head. MRS DUMPTON turns back to HER SON.)
	. . . Look, Terry. Three pounds has been taken from my purse. It's been taken since last night. I haven't taken it out, your Dad hasn't, and I'm sure Lesley hasn't.
TERRY	Are you accusing me?
MRS DUMPTON	I don't know. Am I?
TERRY	You're saying I'm a thief.
MRS DUMPTON	I'm not saying anything. I'm just asking you about my money.

70

80

90

TERRY	I don't know anything about your stupid money. I ain't a thief like my Dad!
MRS DUMPTON	Now that's quite enough of that!
TERRY	I get blamed for everything.
MRS DUMPTON	That's not true.
TERRY	Yes, it is. I'm getting sick of it.
MRS DUMPTON	Terry. Calm down.
LESLEY	Terry had your purse.
MRS DUMPTON	What?
TERRY	Shurrup you!
LESLEY	He did. He had your purse this morning. Before he went to school. I saw him.
MRS DUMPTON	Is this true, Terry?
TERRY	No. She's lying.
LESLEY	I am not.
MRS DUMPTON	I want to know the truth.
TERRY	Just 'cos I won't let you play with my models.
MRS DUMPTON	Terry! I said I want the truth. Did you have my purse? Did you take the money out of it?
TERRY	Why are you asking me? You won't believe me anyway. You'll just believe her. Nobody ever listens to me.
	(He storms out of the room.)
MRS DUMPTON	Terry. You come back here now! Terry! . . .
	(There is silence, so she says)
	. . . Lesley. Go upstairs and tell your brother I want to see him. Now!

10

11

LESLEY	Yes, Mum.	120

(LESLEY goes.)

MRS DUMPTON   That's it, now. I am going to be late. I don't know what's happening. I don't understand it. And where is Arthur? He should be here . . .

(LESLEY comes back. HER MOTHER asks)

. . . Where is he?

LESLEY   Mum. It's Terry . . .

MRS DUMPTON   What about him?

LESLEY   He's smashed all his models.

(Both freeze. Then LESLEY goes away.)   130

SCENE 7

(MRS DUMPTON, alone, faces THE AUDIENCE.)

MRS DUMPTON The final thing was when we had that letter from his school. We knew it was something to do with school, then. Terry had always loved school before. You couldn't keep him away, even when he was ill. We'd had no idea, not until we got that letter, telling us he'd been playing truant. We just couldn't believe it. I'd had enough of it by then. I told his father it was about time he had a word with him.

(She goes. MR DUMPTON then enters, and sits down.)

(After a moment, TERRY enters.)

MR DUMPTON Hallo, Terry.   1

TERRY Hallo.

MR DUMPTON Good day at school?

TERRY All right.

MR DUMPTON What have you been doing today?

TERRY The usual.

MR DUMPTON What's that, then? . . .

(LESLEY comes in. She sits on the floor and plays.)

. . . What are you doing, Lesley?

LESLEY Playing.

MR DUMPTON Go and play somewhere else, will you?   2

LESLEY I want to play here.

MR DUMPTON Play quietly, then . . .

(He says to TERRY)

. . . Well? Go on.

TERRY	What?
MR DUMPTON	You were going to tell me what you've been doing at school today.
TERRY	Just the same old stuff. Maths. English. Science.
MR DUMPTON	Did you do any PE?
TERRY	Oh, yes. We did PE.

30

MR DUMPTON	Anything else?
TERRY	Art. We did Art.
MR DUMPTON	Enjoy it?
TERRY	It was all right.
MR DUMPTON	Good . . .

(A pause. Then MR DUMPTON goes on.)

. . . You're good at reading, aren't you?

TERRY	Yes. Why?
MR DUMPTON	Read this letter for me, will you?
TERRY	Can't you read it for yourself?

40

MR DUMPTON	I want you to read it . . .

(He gives TERRY the letter, and says)

. . . Read it! . . .

(TERRY takes the letter and reads it. Then HIS FATHER asks)

. . . Read it all right? . . .

(TERRY nods. MR DUMPTON says)

. . . So what you've just been telling me has all been a pack of lies. Hasn't it Terry? Hasn't it? . . .

(*A pause.*)

. . . You haven't been at school at all. In fact you haven't   5
been to school this week. That's right, isn't it? Tell me,
Terry!

TERRY   Yes.

MR DUMPTON   Yes. And now I've got to go up and see your Headmistress
tomorrow . . .

(*MR DUMPTON snatches the letter and reads from it.*)

. . . 'I would be very grateful if you would come up to
school and discuss this serious problem with me.' A serious
problem, that's what it is, Terry. It is serious. And I want to
know about it . . .   6

(*A pause.*)

. . . Why haven't you been going to school? . . .

(*TERRY says nothing, so HIS FATHER goes on*)

. . . Look, my lad. I don't intend being made a fool of by
that Headmistress. I want to know why you've been playing
truant. I want a few answers from you. It's about time you
started giving me some . . .

(*A pause.*)

. . . If you don't. I'll give you something to think about!

(*As he raises his hand to hit TERRY, LESLEY sings*)   7

LESLEY   'Humpty Dumpty sat on a wall,
                        Humpty Dumpty had a great fall . . .'

MR DUMPTON   Lesley!

LESLEY   '. . . All the King's horses
                        And all the King's men
                        Couldn't put Humpty . . .'

TERRY	*(To her)* Will you shut up singing that?
LESLEY	No.
TERRY	You'd better or I'll smack you one.
LESLEY	Dad! Terry's going to hit me!

80

MR DUMPTON	Terry! Sit down! Sit down! . . .

(TERRY sits down. Then MR DUMPTON says to HIS DAUGHTER)

. . . Lesley. Get out. Go and play somewhere else. Go on. Now!

(LESLEY stands up.)

LESLEY	I know something you don't know.
MR DUMPTON	What?
LESLEY	Humpty Dumpty didn't fall. He was pushed!
MR DUMPTON	Get out! . . .

90

(LESLEY goes. There is a moment's silence, then MR DUMPTON says)

. . . Now, Terry. Let's try to get to the bottom of this.

TERRY	There ain't nothing to tell.
MR DUMPTON	Yes, there is. There must be. You've never played truant before. You've always liked school.
TERRY	I don't, anymore.
MR DUMPTON	Why not? Is it the teachers? Are they getting on at you? . . .

(TERRY shakes his head. MR DUMPTON goes on)

I know something you don't know . . . Humpty Dumpty didn't fall
. . . *Lesley isn't really saying she knows what's going on with Terry. She's still talking about her nursery-ryhme, and is repeating a joke she's probably heard that day at school, but her words do hit home with Terry and the audience.*

. . . The kids, then? Is it the kids? . . .   10

(TERRY looks up sharply. HIS FATHER continues)

. . . The kids. That's it, isn't it? Am I right? Are they getting at you? Terry?

(A pause.)

TERRY   Yes.

MR DUMPTON   Now we're getting there. I knew it must be something. What is it? Are they making fun of you? Bullying you? Is that it? . . .

(TERRY nods. HIS FATHER goes on)

. . . Why didn't you tell us before? Why've you just let it go   11
on? You should've told us, Terry. Well, never mind. At least we know now. There's nothing for you to be worried about any more. I'll go up to the school tomorrow and get it all sorted out.

TERRY   No! You can't.

MR DUMPTON   I can, and I will. I'm not having you bullied at school. I'm not having them make you stay away. It's got to stop. Now. I want some answers from you, Terry. I want to know all about it. Right, Terry? Right? . . .

(A pause. Then MR DUMPTON says)   12

. . . Now. Start talking.

(They freeze. Then MR DUMPTON and TERRY go away.)

DISCUSSION: As a class, discuss all the things Mrs Dumpton has on her mind in Scene 6, and what her main worries and concerns are.

ACTING: In groups of two, improvise a scene where Mrs Dumpton tells her husband about the events in Scene 6. This can take place later the same evening when Mrs Dumpton has returned home from work, and Terry and Lesley are in bed. It may be that Mr Dumpton has already learned something of what's happened from Lesley.

DISCUSSION: As a class, discuss the reasons you think Terry decides to tell his father he's being bullied in this scene.

WRITING: Write a diary entry for Lesley, where she describes the events that happen in these scenes. Remember that she is a young child.

DISCUSSION: Make notes on the differences in character between Mr and Mrs Dumpton, by placing each name at the top of a page and listing their characteristics beneath, like this:

CHARACTER	NOTES
Mr Dumpton	Mrs Dumpton

Use your notes to discuss as a class which of the two you think is the stronger character.

SCENE 8

(MRS DUMPTON returns, with THE TWO POLICE OFFICERS.)

MRS DUMPTON   That was how we found out, about the bullying at school. It was only yesterday. But it seems like a hundred years ago now. It's them that did it. Them kids. You go to that school and find out. You'll see.

FIRST POLICE OFFICER   It would help if you could tell us the names of these children, Mrs Dumpton.

MRS DUMPTON   Terry wouldn't tell us. No matter how much we asked him to. He was too scared.

FIRST POLICE OFFICER   He never mentioned any of them by name?

MRS DUMPTON   No . . . wait a minute. There was one boy he used to talk about. He can't have been one of that gang, though. I think him and Terry were friends. What was his name now? Sammy. That was it. He used to talk about a boy called Sammy.

FIRST POLICE OFFICER   Sammy what?

MRS DUMPTON   I don't know. Just Sammy.

SECOND POLICE OFFICER   Sammy. Well, that's something for us to go on. Perhaps we can go up to the school and find out who this lad is. Perhaps he'll know who the others are.

FIRST POLICE OFFICER   Thank you for your help, Mrs Dumpton. You've been very kind . . .

(A pause. Then THE FIRST POLICE OFFICER says)

. . . Mrs Dumpton.

MRS DUMPTON	What?
FIRST POLICE OFFICER	You can go home now.
MRS DUMPTON	Oh. Thank you . . .

(She stands, and THE POLICE OFFICERS go. Then she says)

. . . I don't know that I want to. I've been all right here, away from it all. Back at home I've got to try and face it again. Lesley will still be crying. Arthur won't be able to cope. It'll be up to me to try and cope. I'll have to go in and clear his room out. I'll have to wake up in the morning and remember there's one less breakfast to make. I'll have to tell myself it's only my imagination when I hear his footsteps on the front path, coming home from school. I don't know how I'll manage it. But I'll have to. It's always up to me. I have to find ways of carrying on.

(She starts to walk away, but ROSS WEBSTER, a reporter, comes in.)

ROSS	Mrs Dumpton?
MRS DUMPTON	Yes?
ROSS	Ross Webster. *Weekly News*.
MRS DUMPTON	Yes?
ROSS	I'm a reporter. We've heard about your . . . terrible loss . . . and I wondered if you'd like to tell us anything about it.
MRS DUMPTON	Not really. I wouldn't. No.
ROSS	Ah. I know this must be a terrible time for you and, believe

30

40

Weekly News *Could be any town's local newspaper.*

	me, you have my deepest sympathies. Do you have any idea how the accident happened?	
MRS DUMPTON	No.	5
ROSS	Perhaps, then, you could just give us an idea of the events –	
	(MRS DUMPTON shouts)	
MRS DUMPTON	He's dead! What more can I say? My son's dead!	
	(She walks off.)	
ROSS	Mrs Dumpton . . .	
	(A pause. Then ROSS speaks to THE AUDIENCE)	
	. . . People have to know the facts. That's my job. To collect the facts. For a weekly local paper, a story like this is big news. Local tragedy. People want to know who the dead boy was; how it happened; was it an accident, or was there more to it? The facts, and the story behind the facts. That's what people want. That's what you want. You want to read all about it in your local paper. That's what I'm paid for. I'm just doing my job. Reporting the facts. For you . . .	6

DISCUSSION: As a class, discuss whether you think it's right or not for a reporter to interview someone in Mrs Dumpton's situation? Is he intruding on her grief, or does he have a duty to find out 'the facts'? If so, a duty to whom? And what do you think his *real* motives might be?

SCENE 9

(MRS VICKERS enters.)

ROSS	*(To her)* Ah. Mrs Vickers. Ross Webster.	1
MRS VICKERS	Who?	
ROSS	Ross Webster. From the *Weekly News*.	
MRS VICKERS	Oh, yes.	
ROSS	Thank you for offering to say a few words.	
MRS VICKERS	Well, it's the least I can do, isn't it? I mean, I saw it. I saw it all. A terrible thing. I don't know how I'll ever be able to forget it.	

ROSS Perhaps you could start by telling me where you were when the tragedy occurred.

10

MRS VICKERS I was out in the garden, pruning my roses. It's the only chance I get, in the evenings.

ROSS Your garden looks out on to the waste ground, doesn't it?

20

MRS VICKERS Yes. It's not a pretty sight, I can tell you.

ROSS	And what did you see?
MRS VICKERS	Well, I didn't see anything at first. I just heard some kids shouting. They were making a racket. So I had a little look over the fence to see what all the fuss was about. There was this gang of kids all standing around the bottom of the pylon. That big pylon over there.
ROSS	Yes. I see.
MRS VICKERS	Then one of them threw something up into the pylon. One of them whatyoumaycallits. You know. A busby.
ROSS	Busby?
MRS VICKERS	Yes. A busby. One of them round things. People throw them to each other. Made of plastic.
ROSS	You mean a frisbee.
MRS VICKERS	Do I? Well, frisbee, then. One of them threw this busby up into the pylon and it got stuck. Then another one started to climb up after it. I could see it was dangerous. You hear about accidents happening, don't you? I was thinking, he shouldn't be climbing up there, an accident might happen, and just as I was thinking it, it did.
ROSS	What?
MRS VICKERS	It happened. The accident.
ROSS	Could you describe it?
MRS VICKERS	There was a sort of a blue flash. Then a crack. Just as this lad reached his hand up. A blue flash and a crack. It happened very quickly.
ROSS	What did you do then?

3

4

5

One of them whatyoumaycallits 'whatever-you-may-call-its' – Mrs Vickers can't think of the name of the frisbee. In the 1980s, frisbees were a new toy, and Mrs Vickers is of a generation that wouldn't have heard of them before.

MRS VICKERS	I went in straightaway and told Ron. I had to have a lie down as well. I went all faint.
ROSS	But you didn't call the police.
MRS VICKERS	Well, I wanted to at first, but Ron said we shouldn't. He said it would only lead to trouble. Said it was none of our business. He said we should keep quiet about it. I had to agree with him in the end. We didn't want all that fuss with the police and everything.
ROSS	Well, thank you very much for your time, Mrs Vickers. You have been most helpful. 60
MRS VICKERS	Will my name be in the paper?
ROSS	I won't put it in if you don't want me to. You can just be an 'eyewitness'.
MRS VICKERS	Oh, I don't mind, really. It's Vickers. V.I.C.K.E.R.S.
	(ROSS writes this down.)
ROSS	Right. Got that. Thank you again, Mrs Vickers.
MRS VICKERS	Glad to have been of help.
	(She goes.)
ROSS	'The Death of Terry Dumpton. Tragic accident, or deliberate killing?' Yes. It's going to make a good story. 70
	(He goes.)

It's going to make a good story. *By a 'good story', Ross means one that's got all the ingredients of front-page news – tragic death, mysterious circumstances, and so on. Ross' chief interest in this 'good story' is the opportunity it offers him to earn a reputation and to further his career.*

HOT-SEATING: In groups of four, hot-seat the following characters:

		Find out . . .
a)	Mrs Dumpton	why she reacts so angrily to Ross Webster
b)	Ross Webster	what his chief motives are in trying to find out what happened to Terry. Is he really concerned for Mrs Dumpton and her plight?
c)	Mrs Vickers	what her real motives are in speaking to Ross Webster? What kind of person is she?

DISCUSSION: Read through Mrs Dumpton's final speech in Scene 8 again (page 31). Make notes on her thoughts and feelings here, and compare them with those at the start of Scene 3 (page 9). Then discuss as a class how you think she's changed over the course of the six scenes.

ACTING: In twos, improvise a scene between Mr and Mrs Vickers, just after Terry's death, where she tells her husband what she's just seen, and he responds.

SCENE 10

(JIMMY, PETE, SAMMY, KATHY and JANET come in. They stand separately. THE TWO POLICE OFFICERS also enter.)

FIRST POLICE OFFICER	You. What do you know?	1
JIMMY	Nothing. I wasn't there.	
SECOND POLICE OFFICER	You.	
PETE	Me?	
SECOND POLICE OFFICER	Yes, you. Did you know him?	
PETE	Only a bit. Not to speak to. He was a new kid. I just saw him around.	
FIRST POLICE OFFICER	You.	
KATHY	Yeah?	
FIRST POLICE OFFICER	Did you know Terry Dumpton?	10
KATHY	Terry who?	
FIRST POLICE OFFICER	Dumpton.	
KATHY	Never heard of him.	
FIRST POLICE OFFICER	He was at your school. In the same year as you.	
KATHY	Was he? There's a lot of kids at our school. Never heard of him.	

SECOND POLICE OFFICER	You.
JANET	I spoke to him . . . once or twice . . . he was quiet. Kept himself to himself. I didn't have anything to do with him, really.
SECOND POLICE OFFICER	Really?
JANET	Yes.
FIRST POLICE OFFICER	Where were you?
JIMMY	Out with me mates.
FIRST POLICE OFFICER	Can they corroborate that?
JIMMY	You what?
SECOND POLICE OFFICER	Where were you?
PETE	When?
SECOND POLICE OFFICER	When Terry Dumpton died.
PETE	Dunno. Can't remember.
SECOND POLICE OFFICER	Start remembering.
PETE	I'll have a go. I ain't very good at remembering things, though. I suffer from amnesia.

2

3

Can they corroborate that? *'Will your friends support your story?'*

I suffer from amnesia. *Amnesia is a condition whereby the sufferer forgets things easily. No one believes that Pete's being serious when he says this, and he doesn't mean them to.*

FIRST POLICE OFFICER	Where were you?
KATHY	Down the park.
FIRST POLICE OFFICER	Who with?
KATHY	Me mate, Kay. Ask her if you like.
FIRST POLICE OFFICER	What were you doing?
KATHY	Looking for chaps. We didn't find none.
SECOND POLICE OFFICER	Where were you?
JANET	I was out, I think.
SECOND POLICE OFFICER	You think?
JANET	Yes. I was out.
SECOND POLICE OFFICER	Where?
JANET	With Tracey, my friend. We went down the shops to look at clothes. Honest. It's true.
SECOND POLICE OFFICER	I'm sure it is.

(THE POLICE OFFICERS go.)

PETE	(To SAMMY) Sammy. Remember. Don't say anything.
KATHY	(To SAMMY) You don't know nothing. All right? Just keep your mouth shut. It won't just be Stubbs you'll have to worry about.
JIMMY	(To SAMMY) You say anything, and I'll make a right mess of you.

40

50

JANET	*(To SAMMY)* You've got to keep quiet, Sammy. You'll get us all in trouble. Just keep quiet about it. Please.
PETE	*(To SAMMY)* Don't forget, Sammy.
	(PETE goes.)
KATHY	*(To SAMMY)* Keep your mouth shut.
	(KATHY goes.)
JIMMY	*(To SAMMY)* One word . . .
	(JIMMY goes.)
JANET	*(To SAMMY)* Please, Sammy. Let's just try and forget it.
	(JANET goes.)
	(THE POLICE OFFICERS return. They go up to SAMMY.)
FIRST POLICE OFFICER	You!
SECOND POLICE OFFICER	Where were you?
FIRST POLICE OFFICER	You knew him.
SECOND POLICE OFFICER	He knew you.
FIRST POLICE OFFICER	You know what happened.
SECOND POLICE OFFICER	Tell us.
FIRST POLICE OFFICER	Talk.
SECOND POLICE OFFICER	Talk.
	(A pause.)

SAMMY	It was an accident. Sort of. Nobody wanted it to happen. Except Stubbs, perhaps. I wouldn't put anything past Stubbs. He's mad, Stubbs is. Round the bend. It was him who started it all. Started having a go at Terry. I don't know why. He just decided he had it in for him. He'd only been at school for about a week. He was in my class. I'd spoken to him a few times. He seemed all right. A bit quiet, a bit shy. But he was all right. Then Stubbs decided to have it in for him. Nobody knows why. Nobody knows how Stubbs' mind works.

80

(A pause.)

FIRST POLICE OFFICER	Tell us about it, then.

(A pause.)

SECOND POLICE OFFICER	Come on!

SAMMY	All right! I'm trying to remember! . . .

(A pause. Then he continues)

90

. . . It was about a week after he started at school. We was in the playground talking together. And Stubbs and some of the others came up.

(THE POLICE OFFICERS move into the background.)

DISCUSSION: In pairs, discuss how the different gang-members avoid answering the questions put to them by the police, and how this is related to their characters. Also discuss why you think it is that Sammy decides to tell the police what happened, even though he's been threatened by the others.

WRITING: Each of the gang members being interviewed by the police has been asked to write a statement about their whereabouts at the time Terry was killed. Choose one of the gang-members, and write their statement.

SCENE 11

(TERRY comes in and goes to SAMMY.)

TERRY	Crisp, Sammy?
SAMMY	Ta.

(STUBBS, JIMMY, PETE, KATHY and KAY walk up to SAMMY.)

STUBBS	This your new mate, is it, Sammy? This who's been keeping you away from us?
KATHY	Looks like a bit of a drip to me.
PETE	Just right for Sammy. Two drips together.
SAMMY	Leave off, Stubbs.
STUBBS	Who is he?
SAMMY	He's new. Only just started.
STUBBS	I know that. I can see that. I wanna talk to him.

(He pushes SAMMY aside. THE OTHERS encircle TERRY.)

JIMMY	Gi's a crisp.

(TERRY offers the bag. JIMMY snatches it and stuffs the crisps into his mouth. THE OTHERS laugh.)

STUBBS	You're a pig, Jimmy. Say sorry to him for taking his crisps.
JIMMY	Sorry.
KATHY	*(To TERRY)* Where'd you get them trousers from? Off your baby brother? Look at them. Half way up your leg.
KAY	Perhaps they shrunk in the wash.
PETE	Perhaps he shrunk in the wash. There ain't much to him.

STUBBS	*(To TERRY)* You ain't saying much. Why ain't you saying much?
KATHY	Must be dumb.
KAY	Yeah, that's right. Dumb.
PETE	Open your mouth. I said, open your mouth . . .
	(PETE and JIMMY grab TERRY and force open his mouth. PETE goes on.)
	. . . He's got a tongue. I can see it. He should be able to talk.
	(They let TERRY go.)
STUBBS	I know what it is. It's 'cos he don't know us. Never talk to strangers. That's right, ain't it, mate? Never know what might happen to you if you do.
PETE	Drag you away into the bushes.
KATHY	I wouldn't want to drag him nowhere.
KAY	Nor me.
STUBBS	Let's introduce ourselves. Go on.
JIMMY	I'm Jimmy.
PETE	Pete. Very pleased to meet you.
KATHY	I'm Kathy.
KAY	I'm Kay.
STUBBS	And you call me Stubbs. Right. Now you know us. You can start talking.
SAMMY	Stubbs, give it a rest, will you?
STUBBS	You still here?
SAMMY	He ain't done no harm to you . . .
STUBBS	Get lost, Sammy. You ain't wanted our company for the past week, so we don't want yours now.

30

40

KATHY	You heard. Get lost!
JIMMY	Go on!

(JIMMY pushes SAMMY, who moves away and watches from one side.)

STUBBS	Right. You know us now. You know our names. What's yours?
TERRY	Terry.
KAY	Terry what?
TERRY	Dumpton.

(They all laugh.)

KAY	Dumpton! Terry Dumpton! He must live on a dump.
KATHY	What sort of name is that?
STUBBS	Is that your real name?
TERRY	Yes.
STUBBS	Never mind. You can't help it.
PETE	Hey! Terry Dumpton. Humpty Dumpty. Dumpton-Dumpty. That's what his name is. Humpty Dumpty.

(They all laugh and repeat 'Humpty Dumpty!'.)

PETE	Make sure you don't go sitting on no walls. You might fall off.
STUBBS	Right. That's your name from now on. What's your name?
TERRY	Terry Dumpton.
STUBBS	Jimmy. Remind him . . .

(JIMMY grabs TERRY. Then STUBBS says)

. . . That ain't your name. Your name's Humpty Dumpty. Say it, go on. Humpty Dumpty.

TERRY	Humpty Dumpty.
STUBBS	And again.
TERRY	Humpty Dumpty.
STUBBS	What's your name?
TERRY	Humpty Dumpty.
STUBBS	Okay, Jimmy. Loose him now. I think he understands. Do 80 you understand?
TERRY	Yes.
STUBBS	Good. Now listen. Anytime any of us calls you Humpty Dumpty, you answer straight away. Got that?
TERRY	Yeah.
STUBBS	Don't forget. 'Cos we're in charge here. Not the teachers. They think they are, but they ain't. We are.
KATHY	That's right. We're in charge. And don't forget it.
STUBBS	I don't think he will now . . .
	(STUBBS moves away, saying) 90
	. . . Let's go.
	(THE REST move off slowly.)
KAY	Tarra, Humpty Dumpty.
	(As they go, STUBBS speaks to SAMMY.)

STUBBS	Gang's getting together tonight after school, Sammy. Make sure you're there.
SAMMY	I will.
STUBBS	You better be.
SAMMY	Stubbs. What about Terry?
STUBBS	Who?
SAMMY	Terry.
STUBBS	You mean Humpty Dumpty.
SAMMY	Yeah. Can he come along?
STUBBS	I don't want that in my gang. Look at him. He's a bigger drip than you, and that's saying something.

10

(STUBBS goes. SAMMY talks to TERRY.)

SAMMY	They're all right, really. Just having a joke. They like to have a joke. You'll get used to them. It's 'cos you're new. Once you've settled in they won't bother you no more . . .

(TERRY walks off. Then SAMMY speaks to THE AUDIENCE.)   11

. . . He didn't believe me. He knew they wouldn't leave him alone. I knew it, too. I could tell. Stubbs had it in for him from then on. And the others just followed Stubbs. Me too, I suppose. There was something about Terry. I don't know what it was. Something that made you want to have a go at him. He never stood up for himself. He just stood there and took it.

(SAMMY moves to one side.)

SCENE 12

(TERRY enters. So, too, do TRACEY and JANET.)

TRACEY	Is that him?	1
JANET	Yeah.	
TRACEY	I see what you mean.	
JANET	Gorgeous, ain't he?	
TRACEY	Tasty . . .	

(They approach TERRY and prevent him from getting away. Then TRACEY says)

. . . I mean, he's so good-looking. So tall, and strong, and handsome.

JANET	And look at them muscles.	10
TRACEY	He must be really strong.	
JANET	See how he stands and all? Dead cool.	
TRACEY	Yeah. I like them like that . . .	

(She runs her hand through his hair, and says)

. . . You ought to feel his hair.

(JANET strokes his hair.)

JANET	I've gone all shivery.	
TRACEY	Weak at the knees.	
JANET	Tracey. Do you think, if we asked him, he might give us a kiss?	20
TRACEY	I dunno. I daren't ask him.	

JANET	Nor me. I'm too scared.
TRACEY	I bet he wouldn't.
JANET	He might if you asked him.
TRACEY	All right. I'll try. Humpty. Will you kiss me?
	(BOTH GIRLS burst our laughing. SAMMY goes to them.)
SAMMY	*(To THE GIRLS).* Leave him alone.
TRACEY	What do you want?
SAMMY	Will you leave Terry alone?
JANET	Terry? Oh, you mean Humpty Dumpty. I'm afraid I can't. I just find him too irresistible.
SAMMY	You're mad, you two are.
JANET	I think Sammy's jealous.
TRACEY	Yeah, that's right. He wants Humpty all to himself.
	(TERRY is trying to sneak away.)
TRACEY	No, you don't. Come back here.
	(She grabs TERRY and pulls him back.)
JANET	Naughty boy. You mustn't run away from us. We don't want to hurt you. We . . . both . . . love you!
	(They laugh.)
SAMMY	Tell them to get lost, Terry. Tell them.
	(KATHY and KAY are approaching.)
KATHY	Tell who to get lost, Sammy?
SAMMY	Nobody.
KAY	Get lost yourself.
	(SAMMY moves away.)

KATHY	And you two.	
TRACEY	What you mean?	
KATHY	You heard.	
KAY	Get lost.	50
JANET	You can't tell us what to do.	
KATHY	Can't we?	
TRACEY	No.	
KATHY	Want to make something of it?	
	(A pause.)	
KAY	Get lost.	
JANET	We was just going anyway.	
	(TRACEY and JANET walk off.)	
KAY	Mummy's girl.	
KATHY	Stubbs wants his money.	60
TERRY	What money?	
KATHY	The money you owe him.	
TERRY	I don't owe him any money.	
KAY	Yes, you do. A pound, you owe him.	
TERRY	What for?	
KATHY	For not beating you up yesterday. He didn't beat you up yesterday, did he?	
TERRY	No.	

A pound *In 1984, this would have been equal to about £5 today. They're asking him for a lot of money.*

KAY	That's it, then. You owe him a pound.
TERRY	I haven't got a pound.
KATHY	Dear me. He'll have to beat you up today, then.
KAY	I'd better go and tell him the bad news.
	(KAY starts to walk off.)
TERRY	I can bring it tomorrow.
KATHY	How much?
TERRY	A pound.
KATHY	That'll do for tomorrow. There's still today.
TERRY	I'll bring two pounds, then.
KAY	And don't forget yesterday.
TERRY	Three pounds.
KATHY	Four pounds. We want a pound for our trouble.
TERRY	All right. I'll bring in four pounds.
KATHY	All right. I think that'll do. For now, anyway . . .
	(They start to move off. KATHY says)
	. . . Make sure you bring it, Humpty. Else you're gonna get smashed.
KAY	Smashed.
	(They go. Then, SAMMY approaches)
SAMMY	*(To TERRY)* Where you gonna get that money from?
TERRY	That's my problem, ain't it?
SAMMY	You give in too easy.
TERRY	And what happens if I don't? I get beat up. I'd rather give in than get beat up.

7

8

9

SAMMY	But if you keep giving in so easy, it'll just get worse.
TERRY	It's my problem. Anyway, you don't do much to help.
SAMMY	I can't. What can I do?
TERRY	The same as me. Nothing.
	(TERRY goes.)
SAMMY	That's how it went. Every day. Week after week. Just getting on to him, making him bring money, waiting for him after 100 school. They never beat him up or anything. They didn't need to. He did everything they said. I wish he'd have stood up to them just once. That would have been better than giving in all the time. Stubbs got to hate him more and more. Because he took it. He couldn't understand him, you see. He couldn't understand why he just took it all the time.

(SAMMY moves to one side again.)

Stubbs got to hate him more and more. *Hatred isn't usually the feeling a bully has towards his or her victim. It's more often one of contempt. Stubbs' hatred of Terry means there's something in Terry that inspires this powerful emotion in Stubbs, enrages him to the point where he finds himself driven to destroy the thing he hates. Maybe it's the very fact that Terry doesn't resist him, and makes the almost Christ-like act of 'turning the other cheek'. Whatever it is, Stubbs himself is unable to explain it, hence his silence later when questioned by the police. It's not that he won't answer – he can't.*

SCENE 13

(TERRY returns. Then STUBBS, JIMMY, PETE, KATHY and KAY enter. THE MEMBERS OF THE GANG encircle TERRY.)

STUBBS	Your Dad's been in the nick, ain't he? . . .
	(TERRY does not answer. STUBBS goes on)
	. . . Hasn't he?
TERRY	Yes.
KATHY	What for? What was he in for?
TERRY	I don't know.
KAY	Liar.
TERRY	I don't.
STUBBS	Yes you do. You must know.
PETE	They probably put him in because he stinks. Like Humpty stinks.
KAY	Yeah, that's right. Is that why they put him in, Humpty?
TERRY	No.
JIMMY	He does stink, though, don't he? You stink so he must stink.
KATHY	Say it. Go on. Say you stink . . .
	(A pause. Then KATHY continues)
	. . . Go on.
TERRY	I stink.
STUBBS	Now say your Dad stinks. Say it!
	(JIMMY grabs TERRY.)
JIMMY	Say it, Humpty.

1

2

TERRY	My Dad stinks!
	(JIMMY lets go of TERRY. THE MEMBERS OF THE GANG laugh.)
STUBBS	Now. Tell us why your Dad was in the nick.
KATHY	You'd better tell us, Humpty. Or else.
JIMMY	You ain't going nowhere till you've told us.
	(A pause.)
TERRY	He robbed a bank.
	(They laugh.)
PETE	Oh, yeah? Just like Billy the Kid. He come walking into town. Gimme the money or I'll blast your head off.
TERRY	It's true. He did rob a bank. He did.
KAY	What bank?
TERRY	I dunno. A bank.
KATHY	How much did he steal?
TERRY	Ten thousand pounds.
PETE	Ten thousand pounds. It don't look like he did.
TERRY	He hid it. It's in a safe place. He's waiting till it's safe again. Then he's gonna go and get it, and we're gonna be rich.
STUBBS	You're a liar, Humpty. That ain't true and you know it ain't.
KATHY	We don't like liars . . . What did he do, then? You'd better tell us.

Line 30 marks "He robbed a bank." Line 40 marks "He hid it. It's in a safe place..."

Billy the Kid *An infamous outlaw of the American West. The gang would have known about him from cowboy films.*

Ten thousand pounds *A lot of money then, and even more today. But Terry isn't telling the truth. He greatly exaggerates his father's criminal activities in order to gain a kind of respect. Of course, he fails.*

TERRY	He did steal something. He broke into a shop.
JIMMY	How much did he steal?
TERRY	Nothing. The alarm went off and he got caught.
	(All laugh again.)
STUBBS	Is that it?
TERRY	Yes.
STUBBS	Pathetic, that is. Really pathetic. Just like you . . .
	(A pause. Then STUBBS says)
	. . . Come on. Let's go.
	(ALL THE MEMBERS OF THE GANG go, except JIMMY.)
JIMMY	My Dad used to be a boxer. Like this . . .
	(JIMMY shadow-boxes round TERRY, making him flinch. He grabs TERRY and threatens to hit him.
	There is a pause. Then he lets go of TERRY, and says)
	. . . One of these days.
	(JIMMY goes. SAMMY approaches.)
SAMMY	Why'd you let them do it, Terry? Why'd you let them make fun of you like that? . . .
	(TERRY shrugs. SAMMY goes on)
	. . . You ought to do something about it.
TERRY	Like what?
SAMMY	I dunno. Tell somebody.

5

6

Nothing. The alarm went off and he got caught. *Now Terry tells the truth about his father. Like Terry, his father is also something of a loser. The family seems fated to suffer.*

TERRY	Yes, and get my face smashed in. He said . . . Stubbs. If I tell anybody, they'll smash my face. I don't want my face smashed.	
SAMMY	I wish . . . I wish there was something I could do. I'd stand up to them . . . but . . . what can I do . . . ?	70
TERRY	Nothing.	
SAMMY	Perhaps they'll stop soon. Perhaps they'll just get fed up and leave you alone.	
TERRY	You think so?	

(SAMMY shrugs.)

SAMMY	Perhaps.	
TERRY	You know they won't. It's gone on for too long. It'll keep going on. They'll never stop . . .	

(A pause. Then TERRY says)   80

. . . I ain't coming to school tomorrow.

SAMMY	What you gonna do?	
TERRY	Walk round. Go to the park. Anything. But I ain't coming to school. Not any more.	
SAMMY	Somebody'll find out.	
TERRY	I don't care. I just ain't coming . . .	

(TERRY walks off, calling)

. . . See you, Sammy.

SAMMY	Terry . . .	
TERRY	That ain't my name. Ain't you heard? It's Humpty Dumpty.	90

(TERRY goes.

SAMMY faces THE AUDIENCE again. THE POLICE OFFICERS return.)

SAMMY	I know I should've done something. I should've told somebody, tried to get it stopped. They was my mates, though. You can't tell on your mates, can you?
FIRST POLICE OFFICER	I wouldn't call them mates. Would you?
SAMMY	No . . .

(A pause. Then SAMMY says)

	. . . It was Stubbs. He was the one. I was scared of Stubbs. **10** Everybody was. It was like he was . . . I dunno . . . just bad . . . right the way through. He made everybody act like him. You couldn't help it. It was Stubbs.
SECOND POLICE OFFICER	So you didn't tell anybody?
SAMMY	No.
SECOND POLICE OFFICER	Not even when he stayed away from school?
SAMMY	No.
FIRST POLICE OFFICER	Why are you telling us now, then?
SAMMY	I've got to, haven't I? I can't forget seeing him, hanging up there. I can't forget that. I have dreams about it. I wake up **11** and I can still see him. It was my fault. I was just as much to blame. I was there. I never stopped it. I let them do it. I know it's too late now but I've just got to tell. I've got to tell you how it happened. Maybe it'll make the dreams go away.
SECOND POLICE OFFICER	How did it happen, then?

(A pause.)

SAMMY	He stayed away from school. The whole of that week. They didn't seem bothered about it. They never even talked

about him. It was like they'd forgotten all about him. I   120
thought perhaps they had. So I decided to go round to his
house and tell him that everything was all right again, and
he could start coming back to school. I never got the
chance. The day I was gonna do that, Terry's Dad came up
to school. And Stubbs saw his Dad. That's when it all
started again.

(SAMMY and THE POLICE OFFICERS go.)

DISCUSSION: In these three scenes, you witness Terry being bullied in several different ways. First of all, make notes on the different forms of bullying you can find, then, in pairs, discuss which gang-members carry out these acts.

DISCUSSION: As a class, discuss why you think it is that the others, including Sammy, do what Stubbs says. What is it about him that makes the others follow him?

WRITING: Imagine you are Terry, and you keep a diary. Write about the events in these scenes, trying to explain how you feel, why you don't feel able to stop the bullying, what it is you're most afraid of, and what you think is going to happen to you.

ACTING: In groups, improvise one of the scenes where Terry is bullied, changing it so that this time Terry stands up to the bullies. Decide if his standing up to them will make any difference to what happens to him eventually?

DISCUSSION: In pairs, discuss the motives you think the different gang-members might have for bullying Terry. Take each gang-member in turn. Some of them might have different motives than others.

ARTWORK: A gang is held together by a power structure, with the leader, the strongest, at the top, and the weakest at the bottom. Draw a diagram of the power structure of the gang, with Stubbs at the top, Sammy at the bottom, and the others in between:

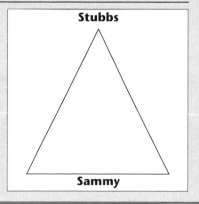

SCENE 14

(THE HEAD TEACHER and ROSS WEBSTER come in.)

HEAD   I'm afraid I haven't got much time to give to you Mr, er . . .

ROSS   Webster. Ross Webster.

HEAD   Mr Webster. My time is rather precious. However, due to the gravity of this case. I will spare you a few moments.

ROSS   I'm very grateful.

HEAD   Any light I can throw on this most tragic accident, I hope will be useful. We are very upset at this school, even though we hadn't got to know Terry very well. But we do take the welfare of all our pupils to heart, Mr Webster, as I'm sure you must realise.   1

ROSS   Of course. Terry hadn't been here long, had he?

HEAD   No. This was his first term. He was a quiet boy, and didn't seem to mix very easily with the other children. From what my staff say, I think he had problems settling in here. We did, of course, take every effort to help him settle in. We are a very caring staff.

ROSS   Had he made any friends here?

HEAD   None that we were aware of. He was rather withdrawn, as I said. I think also he had some family problems. His father, you know, had a criminal record.   2

ROSS   Yes, I knew that. But you don't think that can have had

the gravity of this case *'the seriousness of the situation'. The Head's use of formal language defines her role as an educated person, a teacher, and is used to place her in a superior situation to those with whom she speaks.*

	anything to do with what happened to Terry?
HEAD	Not directly, of course. But one does have to examine all the factors. Terry was obviously rather a problem child. A father who's been in prison, withdrawn, rather uncooperative. They are all, in my experience, contributing factors.
ROSS	To what?
HEAD	To an accident like this occurring, Mr Webster.
ROSS	So you don't think the bullying had got anything to do with it?
HEAD	Bullying?
ROSS	Yes. Apparently Terry was being bullied here at school.
HEAD	Was he?
ROSS	Apparently.
HEAD	Mr Webster, this accusation of bullying has been brought to my attention but I can assure you, as I've assured others, that bullying to the extent you are suggesting was not going on here.
ROSS	You're sure about that?
HEAD	I know my school, Mr Webster.
ROSS	His parents did say that Terry was bullied almost from the first day he came here. And an eyewitness saw a gang of youngsters with him when he was killed.

30

40

contributing factors. *She means that the various elements in Terry's particular family background have much to do with what's happened to him. She implies that the blame lies there, and not in her school.*

Bullying? *At the mention of this word, the Head immediately becomes defensive. Her main concern is to protect the reputation of the school and herself. So, she denies it exists, and will continue to do so, until faced with the truth.*

HEAD	Were they from this school?
ROSS	I don't know.
HEAD	Mr Webster, believe me, if any serious bullying had been going on in the lower school, I can assure you I would have known about it.
ROSS	I see . . .

(A pause. Then ROSS says)

. . . Another thing. Apparently, Terry hadn't been at school during the week before the accident happened.

HEAD	That's right. He had been playing truant. I had to ask his father to come up and see me.
ROSS	Wasn't that on the actual day he was killed?
HEAD	Yes, as a matter of fact it was. I did interview Mr Dumpton that day. But it was a very pleasant meeting, and Mr Dumpton proved to be most helpful.

(ROSS moves back to watch the next scene.)

SCENE 15

(MR DUMPTON enters.)

HEAD	Ah, Mr Dumpton. Thank you for coming to see me. Please sit down . . .	1

(MR DUMPTON sits down. THE HEAD goes on)

. . . I thought it worthwhile us having a chat together to see if we can do something about this problem.

MR DUMPTON   Yes . . . I'd like to talk to you as well.

HEAD   Good. Is Terry at school today?

MR DUMPTON   Yes. I brought him up with me.

HEAD   That's good. I'll have a word with him later.

MR DUMPTON   I'm very concerned about this.   10

HEAD   So am I, Mr Dumpton. Your son hasn't been at this school for very long and, to be quite frank, he doesn't seem to be settling in very well at all. He doesn't even seem to be making any attempt to settle in. And now, with his truancy, I think that if we're not careful, we'll have a very serious problem on our hands.

MR DUMPTON   You've already got one.

HEAD   I beg your pardon?

MR DUMPTON   Terry ain't happy here.

HEAD   So it would appear, despite all the efforts that have been made by myself and my staff . . .   20

MR DUMPTON   I know why. I know why he's been skipping off school.

HEAD	You do? I would be so glad if you would enlighten me.
MR DUMPTON	He's being got at.
HEAD	Got at?
MR DUMPTON	That's right.
HEAD	Surely, Mr Dumpton, you don't mean to suggest that any of my staff . .
MR DUMPTON	Not the teachers. The kids. He's being bullied.
HEAD	Really?
MR DUMPTON	He told me last night. It started as soon as he came here. It's being going on for nearly two months now. Every day. That's why he didn't come to school this week. He's terrified to.
HEAD	Mr Dumpton, this is a very serious accusation you're making.
MR DUMPTON	It's not half as serious as what's happening to our Terry.
HEAD	Did your son tell you who these youngsters were, who were bullying him?
MR DUMPTON	No. He wouldn't tell me their names.
HEAD	I see. Are you sure that your son's telling the truth?
MR DUMPTON	What do you mean?
HEAD	Might he not use a bullying story like this to cover up for his own truancy, to get sympathy for himself and stop himself from getting punished?
MR DUMPTON	My boy don't lie.

if you would enlighten me *'Please tell me what you know.' Her use of language here is sarcastic.*

HEAD	But he couldn't give you any names.
MR DUMPTON	Because he's scared to. They've threatened to beat him up if he tells. Why'd you think he's kept quiet about it all this time?

50

HEAD	I think I'd know if there was any bullying going on.
MR DUMPTON	Terry's telling the truth. I've brought him up to be honest.
HEAD	Oh, yes?
MR DUMPTON	What's that supposed to mean?
HEAD	Nothing.
MR DUMPTON	Anything to do with my record?
HEAD	I wasn't referring to anything, Mr Dumpton. And I don't think we'll get anywhere if we start raising our voices, do you?
MR DUMPTON	It don't look like we're going to get anywhere anyway. Not with your attitude. You just don't want to know, do you?

60

HEAD	I'd be very grateful if you would sit down and lower your voice.
MR DUMPTON	And I'd be grateful if you'd do something about this bullying. Get it stopped. It's your job. That's what you get paid for, ain't it?
HEAD	I will, of course, look into these accusations you've made. But I also think we should both look closely at your son's general attitude and temperament, to see if his problem doesn't lie there.

70

MR DUMPTON	I'll tell you where the problem lies. It's here. You find out

your son's general attitude and temperament *The Head is here saying that much of Terry's trouble comes from his own character and his attitude to school, once again refusing to admit that there might be a problem in the school itself.*

who's bullying Terry. And you get it stopped. Right?

HEAD   There's no need to shout, Mr Dumpton.

MR DUMPTON   Just see that you do it!

(He walks off.)

HEAD   Thank you, Mr Dumpton. Good morning! . . .

(ROSS approaches. THE HEAD TEACHER says)

. . . Yes. Mr Dumpton was most helpful.

ROSS   One more question . . .

HEAD   I'm afraid I don't have any more time to give you, Mr Webster. I've told you all I can about Terry Dumpton, and the whole incident. There isn't anything more to say.

ROSS   Right, well, thanks for your time.

HEAD   No problem at all, Mr Webster. I'm glad to have been of help. We are a very caring school and we have few problems here. I think you'll find that the whole thing has been one of those unfortunate and tragic accidents. But a rare occurrence, I'm sure you'll agree.

ROSS   Yes. Of course.

HEAD   Good morning, Mr Webster.

(THE HEAD TEACHER and ROSS go.)

HOT-SEATING: In groups of four, hot-seat the Head teacher. Try to find out the following:
♦ why she denied the existence of bullying at her school.
♦ why she told Ross Webster her meeting with Mr Dumpton was 'pleasant'.
♦ what she thought of Mr Dumpton and her meeting with him.
♦ what she thinks the explanation is for Terry being killed.

WRITING: Write the report Ross Webster would have made to his editor after his interview with the Head teacher, giving not only the facts, but his views and opinions.

ACTING: In pairs, improvise the scene between the Head teacher and Mr Dumpton, changing it so that Mr Dumpton manages to convince the Head teacher that Terry is being bullied.

SCENE 16

(MRS WILLIAMS and MRS CLARK enter. JANET also enters and stands close by.)

MRS WILLIAMS *(To MRS CLARK)* A terrible thing, really.

MRS CLARK Terrible.

MRS WILLIAMS Do you know her?

MRS CLARK Mrs Dumpton? No.

MRS WILLIAMS I've exchanged a few words. In the launderette. Takes her washing down the same day as I do.

MRS CLARK What's she like?

MRS WILLIAMS All right, I suppose. For having a husband like that.

MRS CLARK Like what?

MRS WILLIAMS Well, you know. He's been inside.

MRS CLARK Has he?

MRS WILLIAMS Yes. That's why they moved here. To try and get away from it. You never get away from a thing like that, though. The Lord piles it on when He has a mind to.

MRS CLARK Piles what on?

MRS WILLIAMS Bad luck. Tragedy. First her husband goes inside, and then this terrible thing happens with her son.

MRS CLARK There'll be something else, then.

 He's been inside. *'He's been in prison'.*

MRS WILLIAMS	What do you mean?	
MRS CLARK	You know what they say. Trouble always comes in threes. She's had two. There's bound to be a third.	20
MRS WILLIAMS	Yes, I suppose so. Poor woman . . .	
	(A pause. Then MRS WILLIAMS says)	
	. . . She wasn't down there yesterday.	
MRS CLARK	Down where?	
MRS WILLIAMS	The launderette. I was down there all morning. Had a big load. Tommy had wet the bed again, so I had all that on top of everything else.	
MRS CLARK	He's not still wetting the bed, is he?	
MRS WILLIAMS	Not so often now. I'm hoping he'll grow out of it soon. Anyway, as I was saying, I was down there all morning, and I never saw her.	30
MRS CLARK	I suppose she doesn't feel up to it. Not with the funeral coming up.	
MRS WILLIAMS	I suppose not. I'm thinking of sending a few flowers. Seeing as I know her.	
MRS CLARK	Our Janet's sending some. She knew the lad, of course.	
MRS WILLIAMS	Did she?	
MRS CLARK	He was in her class.	
MRS WILLIAMS	How terrible for her.	40
MRS CLARK	She was really upset. She couldn't stop crying.	
MRS WILLIAMS	It's a shame.	

Trouble always comes in threes *A common superstition, not really meant seriously. It's part of the light tone of this conversation.*

MRS CLARK	She's a sensitive girl. Always has been. She used to cry all the time as a little girl, over the daftest things. Like when her tortoise hibernated in the compost heap and we burnt it by mistake.
MRS WILLIAMS	I bet she knew the ones that did it as well, then.
MRS CLARK	That gang? She didn't, not really. She's never mixed with that sort. Always kept well away from them. Her father and I would never allow it anyway.
MRS WILLIAMS	I wonder why they did it?
MRS CLARK	Who can tell? It's the way things are these days. Violence wherever you look. It's not even safe to go out on the streets after dark, in case you get attacked or something. I blame it on the television.
MRS WILLIAMS	And the water.
MRS CLARK	The what?
MRS WILLIAMS	The water. All these chemicals they keep putting in it. You don't know what you're drinking. I reckon it's affecting our brains.
MRS CLARK	Yes. I daresay. Janet wanted to go to the funeral, but I said no. I put my foot down. I mean, it's morbid, isn't it? And it isn't as if she knew the lad that well. Hardly ever spoke to him, she said. So I was surprised when she said she wanted to go to his funeral. What on earth for? I asked her. She said she felt she ought to go, show her respect. Show your respect at home, I said. You will not go, so you can get that idea out of your head. I'm not having you going along to that funeral and getting all depressed over somebody's

5

6

I mean, it's morbid, isn't it? *Mrs Clark means she finds Janet's desire to go to Terry's funeral rather gloomy and unwholesome. She's the kind of person who doesn't like to look too closely at the darker side of life. Which is one reason why she has no idea that her daughter has anything to do with what's happened.*

grave, with all that
earth to earth and
ashes to ashes and
everything. It's not
nice, is it?
Anyway, I said
you haven't got
anything black to
wear, and I can't
afford . . .

70

*(JANET interrupts,
shouting)*

80

JANET   Will you shut up?
Will the two of you
just shut up?

(MRS CLARK and MRS WILLIAMS stare at her.)

MRS WILLIAMS   Well!

(She goes.)

MRS CLARK   And what was the meaning of that little outburst, my girl?
What was that all about?

JANET   Just shut up about it!   90

MRS CLARK   I see. Well, we'll see what your father has got to say about
this!

(MRS CLARK goes, followed by JANET.)

DISCUSSION: In pairs, discuss how you learn in this scene that Janet's mother knows nothing of her daughter's involvement in the gang, or Terry's death, and how her view of Janet is different to yours.

ACTING: In pairs, improvise a short scene between Mrs Dumpton and Mrs Williams, in the laundrette, a few days before Terry's funeral.

WRITING: Write down what you think Janet's thoughts are as she listens to her mother and Mrs Williams talking. You could do this in one or more of the following ways.

a)	Write it as a thought-monologue for Janet.
b)	Insert Janet's thoughts into the present scene, in between the dialogue between Mrs Williams and her mother.
c)	Sketch a picture of Janet, with a 'thought-bubble' next to her, containing her thoughts.

SCENE 17

(STUBBS enters, accompanied by THE TWO POLICE OFFICERS.)

FIRST POLICE OFFICER	Stubbs. Stand there.	1

(A pause.)

SECOND POLICE OFFICER
Right. Tell us what happened.

STUBBS
Nothing happened.

FIRST POLICE OFFICER
Don't come that with us. We know all about it. We've been told.

STUBBS
You don't need me to tell you, then, do you?

SECOND POLICE OFFICER
Don't try being funny, Stubbs. This isn't the place for being funny. Things have got past a joke.

FIRST POLICE OFFICER
What we want from you are the facts.   10

STUBBS
The facts.

SECOND POLICE OFFICER
That's right.

STUBBS
Okay. His clothes were too small for him, he had dirty fingernails, and he was a real drip. How's that?

FIRST POLICE OFFICER
We're warning you, Stubbs. You're in serious trouble. There's nobody to help you.

STUBBS
I don't want any help. I don't need it.

SECOND POLICE OFFICER
Did you mean to kill him?

FIRST POLICE OFFICER	Did you do it on purpose?
SECOND POLICE OFFICER	Tell us.
FIRST POLICE OFFICER	Start talking.
STUBBS	I got nothing to say.
SECOND POLICE OFFICER	Stubbs!
STUBBS	Nothing.
SECOND POLICE OFFICER	All right, son. We'll just leave you here for a while to think about it. Think it over. Then we'll come back, and see what you've got to say.
	(THE POLICE OFFICERS go. Then STUBBS speaks to THE AUDIENCE.)
STUBBS	Humpty Dumpty sat on a wall. Humpty Dumpty had a big fall.

SCENE 18

(TERRY enters. STUBBS stands in front of him.)

STUBBS	Hallo, Humpty. Going somewhere?	1
TERRY	Yes.	
STUBBS	No, you ain't. You've been a naughty boy, haven't you?	
TERRY	What do you mean?	
STUBBS	You know what I mean.	
TERRY	No I don't.	
STUBBS	Answering me back, eh? Feeling brave, are you, 'cos you brought your Dad up?	
TERRY	I didn't bring my Dad up.	
STUBBS	Don't lie to me, Humpty. I seen him here this morning. He went into Wilkie's office. You brought him up, didn't you? You told.	10
TERRY	I didn't.	
STUBBS	Why was he here, then?	
TERRY	The Head wrote him a letter. About my not being at school. She said she wanted to see him about that.	
STUBBS	I don't believe you.	
TERRY	It's true!	
STUBBS	You told! And I told you never to tell. You know what'll happen to you now, don't you? You're dead, Humpty.	20
TERRY	I didn't tell. Honest. I didn't, Stubbs. The Head wrote to my Dad.	

(A pause.)

STUBBS	All right, Humpty. I'll give you a chance. A chance to prove if you was lying or not. You'll have to take a little test.
TERRY	What test?
STUBBS	You'll find that out later. You know the waste ground, by the canal?
TERRY	Yes.
STUBBS	Be there tonight. After school.
TERRY	I can't.
STUBBS	What do you mean?
TERRY	I promised my Dad I'd go straight home after school.
STUBBS	Listen, Humpty. If you ain't there tonight, you won't ever be going home again. Got it? Be there.
TERRY	All right. I will.
STUBBS	Go on, then. Push off. And don't forget . . .
	(TERRY goes. JIMMY approaches. STUBBS says to him)
	. . . Jimmy. Go and tell everybody to be at the waste ground tonight, after school. I want everybody there. Everybody. Right?
JIMMY	Yeah. What for?
STUBBS	We're gonna get Humpty.
JIMMY	Get him?
STUBBS	Yeah. His time's up. Go and tell them.
JIMMY	Great. *(JIMMY goes. STUBBS faces THE AUDIENCE again.)*
STUBBS	All the King's horses
	And all the King's men Couldn't put Humpty together again.
	(STUBBS goes.)

SCENE 19

(TERRY enters. There is a pause, then SAMMY enters, running.)

SAMMY	Terry. Go home.	1
TERRY	Get lost, Sammy.	
SAMMY	Go home, Terry. Don't wait round here. You've still got time.	
TERRY	No, I'm staying.	
SAMMY	What for? Are you round the bend? You know what's gonna happen, don't you? Stubbs is gonna get you. I heard Jimmy say. They're gonna get you.	
TERRY	If they're gonna get me, they're gonna get me. I can't keep on running away, can I? I've got to stop and face them some time.	10
SAMMY	Please, Terry. Go. Before it's too late.	
TERRY	It's too late already.	

(STUBBS, JIMMY, PETE, KATHY, KAY, JANET and TRACEY enter.)

JIMMY	I see Sammy got here before us. What you doing here, Sammy?	
SAMMY	Nothing.	
KATHY	I bet he came to warn Humpty. Is that right, Sammy?	
TERRY	No. He didn't. He didn't say nothing to me. He just got here first.	20
KAY	*(To TERRY)* Nobody asked you.	
TERRY	He didn't say anything.	

PETE	He's getting cheeky, Humpty is. He keeps answering back.
JIMMY	Maybe he's gone brave all of a sudden.
STUBBS	Come on, Sammy. Come and join us. Come over with the rest of the gang.
SAMMY	I can't. I got my paper round.
STUBBS	Maybe you ain't one of us any more. Maybe you're with Humpty now. Maybe you want the same treatment he's gonna get.
SAMMY	No . . .
TERRY	He ain't done nothing or said nothing. Leave him alone.
JIMMY	Shut up, you, or I'll shut you up.
JANET	Leave poor Humpty alone. He's nice really, ain't you, Humpty?
	(She strokes his hair.)
TRACEY	I wouldn't do that. He's got nits.
TERRY	No, I ain't!
PETE	See! He did it again. Answered back.
KAY	We'll have to teach him some manners.
KATHY	Yeah. Make him eat dirt . . .
	(She scoops up a handful of dirt, and says)
	. . . Here, Humpty. Eat this . . .
	(TERRY refuses. KATHY shouts)
	. . . I said eat it!
	(KAY grabs hold of TERRY and forces open his mouth. KATHY pushes the dirt into his mouth. They laugh. TERRY splutters).
JANET	Filthy pig. He ate it. I've gone off him. I don't love him any more.

3

4

5

STUBBS	Right, Humpty. Did you tell on us?
TERRY	No.
STUBBS	Did you?
TERRY	No!
JIMMY	I'll get the truth out of him.
	(He grabs TERRY and is about to hit him.)
STUBBS	No. Don't do that.
JIMMY	You said we was gonna get him.
STUBBS	Leave him, Jimmy! We're gonna give Humpty a little test first. If he does it, we'll believe he's telling the truth. If he 60 don't – he's all yours, Jimmy . . .
	(He asks PETE)
	. . . All right?
PETE	Yeah . . .
	(PETE approaches TERRY and says to him)
	. . . See my frisbee, Humpty? My best frisbee, this is. I've had this frisbee for ages. I love it. I'd hate to lose it. I'd go mad if I lost this frisbee. Want to see how it works? . . .
	(PETE throws the frisbee into the air. Then he says)
	. . . Oh, dear. It's got stuck in the pylon. What am I going to 70 do now?
STUBBS	You'll have to get it back, Pete.
PETE	I know. Only trouble is, I'm scared of heights. I get a nosebleed just going to the top of the stairs.
STUBBS	You'll have to get somebody to fetch it down for you then.
PETE	That's right. Who, though?
	(STUBBS points at TERRY.)

STUBBS	Him! . . .
	(There is a pause. Then STUBBS says)
	. . . All right, Humpty? Up you go. Get Pete's frisbee back for him . . 8
	(There is tension. Then STUBBS continues)
	. . . Go on. Climb the pylon. Get it back . . .
	(TERRY stares up at the pylon. STUBBS goes on)
	. . . Perhaps you ain't our mate, then. Perhaps you don't like us at all. That means you're the kind of person who'd sneak on us.
	(He walks towards TERRY.)
TERRY	All right. I'll get it.
SAMMY	Don't, Terry. 9
STUBBS	Shurrup, Sammy.
SAMMY	It's dangerous.
KATHY	You wanna go up there instead?
	(There is a pause.)
STUBBS	Go on.
	(TERRY starts to climb the pylon. Egged on by PETE, THE MEMBERS OF THE GANG start to chant 'Humpty Dumpty!' over and over again, and then shout comments up at TERRY.
	SAMMY runs forward.)
SAMMY	Don't, Terry. Come down. 10
STUBBS	Shurrup, Sammy, unless you wanna go up there after him.
	(The noise continues. Lights suddenly flash on and off. TERRY hangs dead from the pylon. THE MEMBERS OF THE GANG stand in silence.

SAMMY steps forward.)

SAMMY   I'm sorry, Terry. I let you down. I tried, but it wasn't good enough. I'm sorry . . .

(A pause. Then SAMMY says)

. . . Forgive me. Forgive us all.

(The lights fade slowly to black-out.)   110

Forgive me. Forgive us all. *This is a deliberate echo of Jesus' words on the cross: 'Father, forgive them.' To some extent, Terry throughout the play is presented as a kind of Christ-figure, an innocent who dies in order that truth might be revealed.*

HOT-SEATING: In groups of four, hot-seat Stubbs, to see if you can find out why he bullied Terry, and if he planned his death, or if it was an accident.

DISCUSSION: As a class, discuss why you think Terry doesn't go when Sammy tells him to 'before it's too late,' and what you think he means when he says, 'It's too late already.'

WRITING: Write a full character description of Stubbs, showing how you think he's different to the other members of his gang, and what you think it is that makes him different.

ACTING: In groups of three, improvise a scene between one of the gang-members and their parents on the evening that Terry is killed. The parents are asking the gang-member where they've been and what they've been doing. First, think carefully about the character of the gang-member, what their home-life might be like, and what state of mind they might be in in chronological order.

LOOKING BACK AT THE PLAY . . .

1 DISCUSSION: GANGS

People join gangs for many different reasons.

As a class, discuss why people join gangs, and what it is they get out of it.

2 WRITING: CHARACTER

Finish any notes you need to make on the characters in the play to complete your 'character profiles'. Use these to make two lists of characters:

Some characters will fit easily into these lists, others may be more difficult to place. After this, choose one character from each list and write a detailed character-description of them.

sympathetic – we're meant to like them	unsympathetic – we're meant not to like them

3 ARTWORK: SET DESIGN

Although the play is divided into scenes, the writer's intention was that there should be no breaks between scenes, and that action should flow continuously from beginning to end. This kind of production calls for a single, simple set design, which can stand for all the various locations throughout the play.

Given this, how would you design a set for the play? Draw a plan of your set design.

4 DISCUSSION: RESPONSIBILITY

One of the themes of the play is 'responsibility'. Almost every character is, in some way, responsible for what happens to Terry – some, of course, more than others.

In a group, discuss in what way each of the characters is responsible for Terry's death, and which characters, you think, bear the most responsibility.

5 WRITING: A NEWSPAPER REPORT

Write Ross Webster's report for the local paper.

In the report, give all the facts as you've discovered them, and quotes from the various people you have interviewed. As well as Mrs Vickers and the Head teacher, these might include characters such as Mr Dumpton, Mrs Clark, and Sammy. Give your newspaper an eye-catching headline.

6 ARTWORK AND DISCUSSION: STAGING

The play begins and ends with Terry's death on the pylon. This obviously cannot be shown realistically, but needs to be staged to great dramatic effect.

In pairs, discuss how you might show the death on stage, then draw a sketch of your design.

7 WRITING: A MONOLOGUE

Some of the characters speak in monologue to the audience, e.g. Mrs Dumpton, and Sammy. A monologue is when a single character speaks directly to the audience. It is a useful device for letting the audience know how a character feels, and what she or he thinks about events on stage.

Choose a character from the play, and write a short monologue for them. Before you start, decide at what point in the story they're speaking, what the events are they're describing, and how they feel.

8 DISCUSSION: COMEDY

Although the play deals with a serious subject, some of the scenes, characters and dialogue are deliberately comic.

First of all, in pairs, find what you think are the comic moments in the play, then, as a class, discuss why comedy is used, and what purposes you think it serves.

9 WRITING: CHARACTERS

In any play, not all the characters can have equal weight. Some are more central to the story, while others are less involved. The cast can therefore be divided into 'major' and 'minor' characters. Write out lists:
Give reasons for your opinion.

Major characters . . .	Minor characters . . .
....	....
....	....

10 WRITING AND DISCUSSION

In the play, the story is presented in a series of flashbacks. Events are not presented in chronological order – in the order they happen. Scene 3, for example, takes place after Terry's death, whereas Scenes 4, 6 and 7 all take place some time before. Similarly, although Scene 19 with Terry's death is the last scene in the play, the events portrayed in Scenes 9 and 14 – the Ross Webster scenes – actually take place after it.

Looking at the events as they occur in time, list the scenes of the play in strict chronological order. The first and last are done for you.

1st	Scene 11
2nd	Scene 4
3rd	Scene 12
....	....
....	....
18th	Scene 17
19th	Scene 16

In groups, discuss why you think the writer decided to present the events in this way, rather than presenting them in chronological order.